GROWING TREES FOR PROFIT

CRAIG WALLIN

TABLE OF CONTENTS

INTRODUCTION — 5

CHAPTER - 1
8 WAYS TO GROW TREES — 9

CHAPTER - 2
WHAT YOU NEEDS BEFORE YOU START GROWING TREES — 15

CHAPTER - 3
STARTING YOUR TREE NURSERY — 25

CHAPTER - 4
TREES NURSERY SUPPLIES — 31

CHAPTER - 5
CONTAINER TREES — 39

CHAPTER - 6
LANDSCAPING TREES — 45

CHAPTER - 7
FRUITS TREES — 55

CHAPTER - 8
NUT TREES — 61

CHAPTER - 9
VALUE - ADDED TREES (BONSAI) — 67

CHAPTER - 10
HIGH - VALUE TREES PRODUCTS — 79

CHAPTER - 11
JAPANESE MAPLES — 85

CHAPTER - 12
CHRISTMAS TREES — 91

CHAPTER - 13
SELLING YOUR TREES — 103

CHAPTER - 14
SETTING GOALS — 107

CHAPTER - 15
BUSINESS BASICS   111

CHAPTER - 16
HELPFUL RESOURCES FOR
TREES GROWER   115

CONCLUSION   119

INTRODUCTION

Trees have consistently been emblematic for us; they mean numerous things and as of late represent the progressions we are encountering on our planet. A Tree frequently represent insight, expectation, mysticism, but in the 21st Century, they are turning into an image to the natural demolition that we are confronting today.

At the point when we imagine that on the planet just 5% of the regular woodland remain, and in many arising nations, rainforests are proceeding to be chopped down. It is peculiar that a considerable lot of us, utilize the images of the tree as an indication of insight, and expectation.

Planting a tree is a deep-rooted venture. How well this speculation develops relies upon the sort of tree chose and the planting area, the care gave during planting, and the subsequent care in the wake of planting. Getting your new tree looking solid so far will enable the tree to develop to its full measure and guarantees it will give ecological, financial, and social advantages all through its lifetime.

Notwithstanding, growing trees for benefit is an ideal low maintenance or full-time business for any individual who needs to work for themselves and appreciates being outside working with plants. Trees are a productive and inexhaustible asset that can be filled in a little patio or land. The best part is that trees are not an occasional harvest like blossoms or vegetables. On the off chance that your blossoms or reaped vegetables do not sell, you do not make anything. All things being equal, trees simply continue growing, so you can sell the bigger trees one year from now for more cash.

That is perhaps the best motivation to develop trees, their value continues expanding every year. You can begin a tree growing business with a little venture of cash as meager as two or three hundred dollars. You needn't bother with a degree in agriculture either some presence of mind and the capacity to learn as you develop.

Since little scope tree growing takes only a couple hours seven days, most little producers are seasonal workers. Tree cultivating is an extraordinary method to procure additional pay for the individuals who appreciate seeing plants develop. In the event that you have ever contemplated beginning a little tree nursery, or tree cultivating.

ADVANTAGES OF GROWING TREES

- Growing trees can be a sound budgetary choice. In any case, more than that, it very well may be a moral activity.

- Each tree you plant will deliver oxygen and sequester carbon from the environment, helping in the battle against an unnatural weather change.

- Carry downpour to the land and assume a pivotal part on the planet's water cycle.

- Use sustainable resources and catch and store energy.

- Store water and balance out the dirt.

- Ensure the dirt and increment encompassing soil ripeness.

- Give biomass to fuel needs and ripeness.

- Give some shade from the sun.

- Give wind breaks.

- Channel residue and clean the quality of other airborne toxins.

- Give significant wood, fruits, nuts, blossoms, prescriptions and different resources for people.

- Give feed, territory and different resources for other livestock and untamed life.

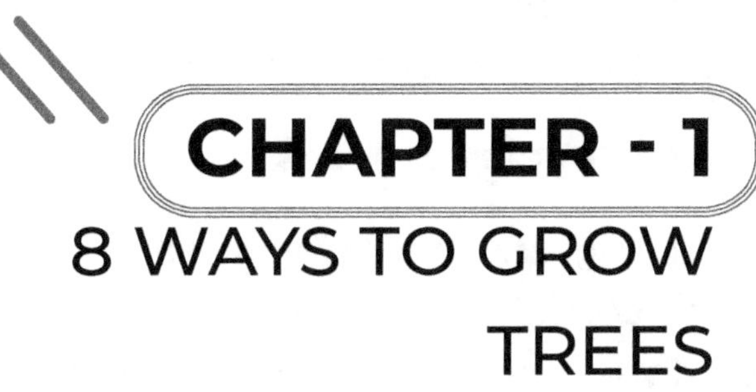

CHAPTER - 1

8 WAYS TO GROW TREES

Planting another tree is something other than burrowing an opening and adding something to the earth. A tree is a drawn-out speculation. It is essential for the general check allure of your home, it can give shade and energy reserve funds, and trees are likewise an unimaginably significant piece of our biological system.

The enormous size trees are advantageous for our environmental framework, yet they are outwardly engaging and help to build the control allure of your property. At the point when you move and move into another house, at that point you will see that your yard looks void in light of the fact that there is no tree or your trees are little.

Moreover, contingent upon your yard's conditions, one types of tree might be a superior decision than another. For instance, oak trees like a specific level of sharpness in the dirt, while willow trees love an unnecessarily soggy soil. Different things property holders should seriously think about is the size, protection, shade, and shading that a tree may offer. in the event that you are determined to planting something yourself, here are some bit by bit headings on the best way to improve:

1. Plant Right Species of Trees

Prior to planting any tree in your yard, guarantee that you pick the correct types of trees. Certain tree species fill great in your yard. Then again, certain species are bad for your region and encompassing environmental conditions. The various trees need an alternate measure of water, daylight, temperature level, and soil type.

As per the examination directed by specialists, the climatic conditions needed by various trees are unique. In the event that you need that the tree in your yard develops taller, at that point you should decide the dirt kind in your yard and afterward select the correct tree species appropriately. A tree whose developed stature is around 50 feet will develop rapidly as contrast with the tree with 15 feet developed tallness. The tree that becomes quickest are more vulnerable and can't withstand weighty breezes and tempest. The quickest developing trees have a short life expectancy as contrast with the moderate growing trees.

2. Properly Plant Trees

While planting trees, you should burrow an opening whose profundity is multiple times the tree roots and width are more than the tree root ball. You should fill the opening with a blend.

This blend ought to be included half soil and rest with

great fertilized soil. The gardening soil is involved the nutrients that will help in improving the development of trees. You ought to guarantee that you give satisfactory water to your trees routinely.

3. Sufficient Water to Tree Roots

Offering a decent measure of water close to a tree isn't gainful. It is so on the grounds that the majority of the water will flee. There are various ways for ideal watering. For example, a dribble water system framework, tree watering packs, and so on They help in delivering a decent measure of water to your trees for an extensive stretch. It is a great idea to deliver the most extreme measure of water to your tree roots. Along these lines, a root water system framework is highly proficient. In this framework, the root water system stake is burrowed around the trees and lines are introduced 3 feet down. The lines help in delivering the necessary measure of water to your trees. This framework will help in deliver giving water legitimately to the foundations of trees.

4. Give Required Fertilizer

Manures are significant for the development of trees; in this way, you ought to give a satisfactory measure of right compost to your trees. You can utilize natural compost so that there should be no unsafe impacts of manures. You can plan natural composts at your home or buy them from a close by store. Prior to applying composts, you should peruse all the directions referenced on the bundle.

5. Mulching to Keep Soil Moist

Mulching is a cycle where wood chips are spread around the trees. Mulching helps in holding great dampness levels in the dirt. This will at last assistance in improving the development of trees. Mulching is highly useful during sweltering mid-year days. Besides, mulch likewise decreases the development of undesirable plants around the tree. Ensure you don't pile up wooden pieces around the tree on the grounds that piling up will prompt terrible outcomes.

6. Dispose of Weeds

You ought to limit the development of undesirable plants around the tree. These plants will remove a tremendous measure of water and nutrients that are needed by your trees.

Consequently, in the event that you need that your tree develops taller and quicker, at that point you ought to dispose of weeds or undesirable plants around the tree.

7. Guard Your Trees

You ought to keep trees in your yard from a lawnmower or weed remover. These devices can harm your trees and can prompt irritation or contagious pervasion. In addition, the harmed tree devours an immense measure of energy for recuperating. Hence, it prompts the moderate development of trees and furthermore influences the tallness of trees. In this manner, you ought to keep your trees from any slice due to lawnmower.

8. Tree Trimming

At the point when your braid begins growing and acquired great stature, at that point you ought to do tree managing. This will help in eliminating infections or broken pieces of the tree. You should call the tree specialist co-op and routinely trim trees to reestablish solid and ideal development of trees in your yard.

CHAPTER - 2
WHAT YOU NEEDS BEFORE YOU START GROWING TREES

1. Measure of water for trees

A. Equilibrium is significant in all parts of your life. Shockingly, this incorporates tree care!

Watering the perfect sum is fundamental to keeping your trees solid and sound. Both watering excessively or excessively little can be unsafe.

On the off chance that the leaves are earthy colored on the edges and are hanging or withered, your tree is not getting enough water. Then again, green leaves that effectively break could mean you are over-watering.

The measure of water your tree needs changes relying upon how old it is so guarantee you know the ideal sum.

B. Youthful trees need more care and consideration for the initial 1-2 years. During this time, trees center around growing their underlying foundations, which is the reason you will see minimal over the ground development. The enchantment is occurring underground!

By furnishing the tree with enough water, you are developing further, generous roots while additionally advancing stem and leaf development.

On the other side, in the event that you do not water your recently planted tree enough, your tree will create negligible roots, experience the ill effects of covering dieback and take more time to build up.

To set your new tree up for progress, give 20 gallons of water week by week. The simplest method to do this is to pour a 5-gallon pail over the trickle zone, the piece of ground the shelter covers, multiple times.

Something else, leave a sprinkler or hose out somewhere in the range of 30 minutes to 2 hours. To pinpoint precisely how long, place a vacant soup can under the tree. Time what amount of time it requires to load up with two crawls of water, at that point water for that long later on.

C. The underlying foundations of a develop tree have just spread out, so it does not require as much consideration! Plan to water develop trees 1-2 times each month.

In light of the measure of downpour and warmth levels in your district, this may change. Also, it is consistently keen to water all the more regularly when there is a dry season.

To check whether your tree needs water, stick a long screwdriver into the soil—in the event that it is difficult to push in, water.

Attempt profound root watering to water the tree less regularly while guaranteeing it gets the best possible measure of water!

2. Instructions to Choose the Right Space to Plant A Tree

Planting a tree is a magnificent thing. Trees can ration energy, dispel any confusion air, and secure property. Trees can give food, save soil, and add value. There are a large number of things trees can do, beyond any reasonable amount to list here.

In any case, not all trees are similarly appropriate for each planting area. While considering new tree planting around your private or business property, tree choice and situation are among the main elements when arranging your landscaping exertion. So significant actually, that the effects might be long lasting the same number of trees (developed with care) will probably outlive the individuals who planted them.

Planting in an area that favors the tree and the land owner is pivotal.

» The Right Tree for the Job

What will be the capacity of the tree to be planted? An enormous verdant tree almost a structure can give cooling conceal from the blistering summer sun and, if deciduous, will lose its leaves in the fall permitting the colder time of year sun to help warm a home, lowing energy utilization simultaneously.

An evergreen with its thick all year foliage planted close to the border of a property can add to a home or business' security just as give much-invited cover during breezy days. Street trees planted along streets can decrease downpour spillover, asphalt glare, and improve the general property value and presence of an area.

The shape or type of a tree will supplement the picked work and even lessen upkeep costs. There are many structure and size mixes to pick from. A line of segment like evergreens may give an ideal protection divider between properties or an enormous adjusted covering can conceal your home or square undesirable brightening from passing vehicles or street lights.

» The Right Tree for the Space

Trees can possibly give their ideal capacity whenever planted in the correct area, a spot where they won't meddle with or harm encompassing structures or framework. Ground breaking will forestall long haul issues.

Consider tree size – When choosing the correct area for a tree, think about the expected tallness and width of the tree at development. Will the absolute stature block perspectives or danger contact with electrical cables running into a structure? Will the spread of a tree's covering meddle with a home's rooftop or could a broad root framework harm underground utility lines or other hardscape and foundation?

It is essential to consider the complete actual space a tree may develop into. You do not need a tree planted today to harm underground pipes or represent a fire peril not far off.

Consider tree litter – If you are thinking about a deciduous and additionally fruit-bearing tree, you should recall what the tree may abandon season after season. Falling leaves and trash can jumble up pools and lakes as minor bothers and can hinder downpour drains causing flood or present fire risks best case scenario.

A fruit-bearing tree then again, while additionally making a wreck of trash around the tree, can pull in creatures, creepy crawlies, and other undesirable nuisances. In the event that excessively near your home or business, these bugs will probably discover their way inside making totally new issues once inside.

Think before you burrow – Always, have your neighborhood service organization distinguish and mark the areas of all utility lines prior to burrowing. There will probably be gas, electric, water, and sewer lines going through your yard and diving prior to checking could bring about genuine injury or exorbitant fixes.

Likewise, recall that a tree's root framework can develop to coordinate the circuit of the tree's covering and conceivably harm underground utilities. Your nearby service organization can assist you with deciding your yards freedom necessities.

3. Tree Planting Permit

A Tree Planting permit is needed to plant trees and shrubs in the public option to proceed (ordinarily the territory between the walkway and the street or nonpartisan grounds). You should submit plans for the trees as well as shrubs planned to be planted and the permit is for nothing out of pocket. Candidate must consent to water the tree for one year. There is a base caliper (width of tree) size of 2 inches and a groin tallness prerequisite of 5 feet.

Expenses - Free

Required Documents/Steps - Submit Tree Planting permit application and site plans

Site Plans – these plans need not be proportional however should have measurements noted on the arrangement for such things as carports, posts, get bowls, width of line. strip, walkway width, good ways from different trees.

Giving Agency - Parks and Parkways

4. The 10 Commandments of Tree Planting

In addition to the fact that trees bring happiness to a garden they clean the air, give oxygen, welcome natural life and shade the garden. Yet, planting a tree is not as straightforward as delving an opening and tossing in the tree.

1. Pick carefully

The motivation behind why you need to plant a tree will decide the kind of tree you ought to pick. Basic purposes incorporate protection, feel, shade, windbreak or to make a fledgling living space. Do your exploration and address your neighborhood nursery on the grounds that your ultimate objective will affect the reasonableness of various trees.

2. Area, area

Trees need a lot of space to create both their root frameworks underground and branches over the ground. Try not to plant trees close to phone lines, structures or in little regions.

3. Soil test

There is a familiar axiom that the way to growing a plant is to placed a 50-penny example in a $5 opening. The dirt is the main pointer of whether your tree will develop well so ensure you test the region's reasonableness. Burrow a 30-centimeter opening and fill it with water. Leave it short-term and verify whether it is unfilled in the first part of the day. On the off chance that it has depleted not exactly a centimeter 60 minutes, the dirt has a seepage issue.

4. Burrow persistently

The general guideline is to burrow an opening twice as wide as the root ball however multiple times as wide is shockingly better. The profundity of the opening ought to be close to the tallness of the root ball to forestall settling.

5. Plant appropriately

Plant trees when climate is cool and overcast, yet not breezy. Ensure the best side of the tree is confronting the heading you need prior to scooping refill into opening until roots are covered. Check regularly all through to guarantee trunk is straight.

6. Prepare economically

Compost is just of negligible advantage at planting time, and it can even be destructive to roots so it is ideal to maintain a strategic distance from. Stand by until the next year to prepare youthful trees softly.

7. Water well

When all is said in done, water new trees two times per week yet soon after planting you might need to water each day for half a month. Try not to permit roots to dry out in any case trees may bite the dust. To check if your dirt is very much watered, utilize a scoop to burrow the edges of the territory. Soil that is soggy and holds together when pressed needn't bother with more water.

8. Avoid the pruning

Recently planted trees need just insignificantly pruning. Just prune dead, infected or harmed branches.

9. Stake reasonably

Just stake trees that are enormous or cannot withstand wind. In the event that your tree needs marking, drive stake through root ball into ground underneath. Stakes ought to be tied freely and eliminated when not, at this point required (a few seasons). Trees that are marked too firmly or for a really long time will not grow appropriately.

10. Must mulch

A recently planted tree needs mulch. A 10-centimeter layer of mulch around the base of tree will keep gets rid of, decrease water misfortune and protect the dirt.

CHAPTER - 3
STARTING YOUR TREE NURSERY

Tree nurseries offer homegrown and outlandish tree varieties to property holders and business visionaries hoping to tidy up their properties. These nurseries range from little organizations that attention on certain tree varieties to full-scale tree nurseries with delivery and landscaping administrations accessible. The accomplishment of a tree nursery relies upon provoking an interest among manufacturers, engineers and families in the encompassing network. Your tree nursery needs to connect with the network and exhibit what specialty your business dispatches to make due past the primary summer.

Analyze the degree of interest for your tree nursery's administrations in your field-tested strategy. Rundown each landscaper, building temporary worker and home improvement store in your general vicinity to show the quantity of forthcoming clients. Commit space in your field-tested strategy to accommodating your beginning up financial plan with the expenses of discount trees, compensation and different expenses over the main year.

Buy a vacant property outside of your city to give your tree nursery space to extend. Your tree nursery should be found near townhouse, condo and business advancements to exploit landscaping needs by developers. Search for plots that are pitched somewhat downhill from the passage to build water course through a water system framework.

Measure the cubic film of your nursery zone and record for strolling space between trees when requesting discount trees. Get saplings and seeds from your distributer to offer local trees to clients.

Outfit your tree nursery with tree clippers, hoses, wheel carts and tree stockpiling. Ask about blossoms, packs of soil and other extra products that you can show in your retail facade as drive buys. Introduce a capacity shed at the back of your property to guard abundance supplies from the components.

Purchase a pickup truck that you can use to drop off trees to clients. Contact nearby printing and custom auto shops to locate the best arrangements on decals with your nursery name and telephone number on the truck.

Utilize a small bunch of full-time and low maintenance laborers to staff your tree nursery. Your checkout counter can be staffed by a solitary position occupied by low maintenance day and night staff member. Recruit a modest bunch of nursery staff members who can manage developed trees, assist clients with finding the correct varieties and burden up trucks for deliveries. In the event that your nursery offers landscaping administrations, recruit a group of summer laborers who can deal with the majority of your landscaping ventures.

Set up your tree and embellishment costs prior to opening a tree nursery. Make valuing for singular trees and mass buys to urge organizations and designers to secure many trees with each outing. Compute the time-based compensations of your landscaping groups and add a slight markup when estimating your delivery and transplant administrations.

TIPS FOR CHOOSING THE RIGHT SIZE TREE FOR YOUR LANDSCAPE

Deciduous trees are an adaptable, appealing and dynamic component for use in any landscape plan since they are incredible parts in the climate. These are the trees that have a trunk underneath and a shelter above. They lose their leaves in winter and experience a few changes over the seasons. They make natural surroundings, characterize space, and offer screening and shade. They manufacture character to the landscape with a wide range of surfaces and shadings. There is a wide assortment to browse in any planting zone permitting you to coordinate size, shape and similarity to your area and undertaking.

THREE CRITICAL CONSIDERATIONS FOR TREE SELECTION

Choosing the correct tree type (family and species) for your property requires knowing something about the agricultural parts of the tree. What does it like/need, what are its best highlights, what may hurt the tree later on, how might you help care for it?

Pick the shape and type of the tree to supplement the

look or capacity you want and drive the general character you are focusing for the landscape.

Distinguish the right arrangement of your tree for present goals while considering the future effects of that position numerous years from now.

Appropriately taking care of the over three choice models will fundamentally decrease long haul support costs while expanding the trees' viability and value as a necessary portion of a landscape plan.

WHAT TO LOOK FOR IN NURSERY TREES

While choosing a tree from a nursery, think about its general wellbeing. Check over the roots, top to trunk qualities, foliage and branch dispersion and be certain it is liberated from injury and irritations.

Regardless of whether you are searching out a container-developed tree or a balled and pod lapped, search for the accompanying:

Next to zero scarring on the storage compartment – from the appendages to the root flare

Insignificant dead branches all through the crown (ideally none!)

A general sound appearance—dodge a pounded looking tree

No blotches or openings on the leaves (vermin or sickness)

A solid focal trunk as the primary component. Dodge a twofold trunk. Branches can be pruned after some time to adjust the appearance or weight of the tree.

CHAPTER - 4
TREES NURSERY SUPPLIES

Experts realize that nurseries need an enormous assortment of provisions to keep their stock growing, perfectly coordinated, and solid. Pots and plate are required for seedlings and plants; labels and marks are needed for monitoring stock; manures, bug sprays, and fungicides are expected to keep plants solid and illness free.

Adding trees to your landscape is one of the most fulfilling and emotional changes you can make to your property. Having the instruments to make it simpler, and to guarantee fruitful watering and mulching conditions will guarantee that your speculation merits the exertion!

1.   Growing Trees in Containers

Planting trees in containers is getting more mainstream, particularly in landscapes with almost no external space. You needn't bother with an enormous bit of property to grow a tree. In the event that you have a yard, porch, or gallery, you can grow a tree in huge container. Container-developed trees can be utilized to outline gateways or to give intriguing central focuses. They are appropriate to little spaces in the landscape, for example, porches and decks and can be utilized close by other container-developed plantings also.

Picking a Container for Your Tree Trees can be planted in ordinary, moveable containers just as in enormous, perpetual planters. Containers and planters for landscape trees are accessible in various styles, shapes, and shadings. Containers ought to consistently supplement their environmental factors just as the trees that are set in them. The container should be huge enough to oblige the tree.

In this way, the develop size of the tree ought to be considered to pick a container with satisfactory space to oblige both the growing tree and its foundations. Containers ought to likewise be as wide as they are high to give the most ideal protection to the roots. The general load of a container is significant as well, and this ought to be thought about also. Not exclusively is simply the heaviness of the container a factor, yet consider how much weight the dirt, tree, and water will add to it, particularly if the container will be utilized in territories, for example, overhangs or housetops, where auxiliary weight limit might be an issue.

2. Fertilizing Potted Plants

Regardless of whether you are growing inside or out, compost is basic to the accomplishment of container gardens. The least demanding approach to fertilizing pruned plants is by setting up a nutrient arrangement and pouring it over the dirt blend. The compost is consumed by the roots and rapidly adds what is absent from the current soil. Regardless of whether your preparing blend is amazing as it so happens, it will before long get exhausted of nutrients as they are continually spent by plants and filtered out by watering. The quicker a plant develops the more manure and water it will require. Therefore, as watering is expanded so is draining and nutrient misfortune.

Whenever you have chosen a manure (ensure you utilize a natural one!), you should apply it about once like clockwork for container developed plants. This accepts that you are growing in a high quality, fertilizer rich preparing blend that will help hold nutrients. All things considered; a few gardeners want to treat with a powerless nutrient arrangement each other time they water. On the off chance that this is your inclination, try to use around 1/5 the sum called for on the mark.

3. Plant Labeling

Plant names are your key to progress with picking and growing plants. On the off chance that you don't see all the things you see on a name; you are in good company. Disentangle the puzzle of plant name language and remove the mystery from choosing and siting plants in your yard.

The Basic Building Blocks

Plant names might be extraordinary, yet frequently they contain comparable data. Here are a portion of the regular words you will see on plant names and what they intend to you.

> » **For what reason would it be a good idea for me to mark my trees?**

- Association. Recognize what is growing on your property.

- Wellspring of significant data, for example, where tree was bought and date planted.

- Guests can appreciate comprehending what is growing in your yard.

- At the point when you move or pass on property, new proprietor comprehends what is growing.

> » **What ought to be remembered for tree name?**

- Type and assortment of tree

- At the point when tree was planted

- Where tree was bought

- Rootstock (whenever known)

- Some other appropriate data you might want

> » **In what manner would it be advisable for me to name my trees?**

There are a few distinct strategies. Every technique requires upkeep. Choose which strategy or mix of strategies will work for you.

- Name in tree on branch.

- Aluminum markers are effectively decorated with a ball-point pen.

- Use wire to balance an enormous circle around a platform branch. Try not to append to primary branch, as it could support (choke) principle tree whenever left unattended for quite a long time.

Merits: Easy to utilize. Waits in tree.

Demerits: Could support branch, must release latch as tree develops.

- Name for tree in ground.

- Utilize an aluminum marker and emblazon with ball point pen.

Merits: Easy to utilize. Simple to see which trees have been marked.

Demerits: Can be effectively lost or moved.

4. Watering Systems

Plant water system frameworks are a basic apparatus to help the effective development and improvement of plants and trees. By introducing a plant watering framework inside a planter, bed or show territory you are basically giving the right measure of water direct to the plant's underlying foundations and giving it the best beginning throughout everyday life.

5. Mist Propagation System

Moistening is a procedure for limiting plant dampness misfortune by controlled occasional wetting of the foliage of cuttings which are being established. This method is useful for establishing verdant cuttings; be that as it may, delicious plants are typically not put under fog.

Consistent clouding has been fruitful with a couple of plants; however, results are commonly better with irregular moistening. Steady clouding squanders water, filters nutrients from the leaves, and diminishes soil temperatures which, thus, limits root improvement. Fog beds can be utilized in nurseries all year or during the growing season for nursery stock.

HOW WOULD I USE MISTING TO PROPAGATE TREES?

There are two general approaches to spread trees - by seeds or cuttings. Cuttings are a technique for cloning, bringing about a tree that is hereditarily indistinguishable from the parent plant. This is fundamental while spreading a chose cultivar to imitate its attributes. Animating the development of roots from a stem-cutting of a tree is supported by the glow and high dampness of a moistening chamber.

TREE CUTTINGS AND MISTING

Moistening keeps the tissues of a removing from drying before new roots have framed. This technique is viable with evergreen and deciduous trees; in spite of the fact that the last is likewise engendered by cuttings of lethargic wood that do not need clouding. The ideal slicing is 4 to 6 creeps long and no thicker than a pencil. The growing tips of branches are commonly too delicate to even consider surviving and structure roots in the wake of cutting, yet the rest of any branch down to where it becomes solid and woody is reasonable material for making cuttings.

6. Hoop House

A hoop house is basically a modest nursery utilizing a plastic rooftop over twisted metal or PVC tubing. For an unassuming venture of only a couple hundred dollars and a day or two of your opportunity to gather it, you can make a "growing machine" that can without much of a stretch compensation for itself in only one growing season.

A circle house gives you a controlled climate that can give ice security, wind insurance, mugginess control and bug control. Since a hoop house can likewise expand the growing season in spring and fall, you can become bigger, more beneficial plants and more benefits for your nursery.

The choice of plants or vegetables for growing inside a circle house relies generally upon your decision, atmosphere, and market interest (If you are growing for the market).

You can without much of a stretch become the vast majority of the vegetables inside your circle house. Greater part of the hoop house gardeners develops tomatoes which is a high-value crop. Additionally, tomatoes you can undoubtedly develop normal veggies like cucumbers, spinach, eggplant, ringer peppers, lettuce, broccoli, melons, summer squash, and so forth inside your hoop house. You can likewise develop fruits like raspberries, citrus, strawberries, peaches, and grapes. At last, in spices, you can develop chives, Basil, Dill, Parsley, Mint, Chamomile, and Cilantro in your band house.

CHAPTER - 5
CONTAINER TREES

PICK THE RIGHT TREE FOR PLANTING IN CONTAINERS

In any event, when space is restricted, getting a charge out of specific types of trees is as yet conceivable in the correct containers. Numerous individuals that live in condos or townhouses have restricted outside space. Normally this open-air space comprises of a little porch, deck, or even only an overhang, and utilizing this space is critical. Planter boxes loaded up with annuals and other blooming plants make an incredible appearing, however a container tree adds a strong visual anchor when restricted in space.

Not all trees are appropriate for containers. While choosing a tree for a container, one must pick an animal variety that will withstand extraordinary temperature changes and can prosper in restricted soil. Before we will tree choice, we should initially pick an appropriate container for the area.

The primary inquiry to be addressed is will the container tree should be moveable or will it be a perpetual position? In the event that there will be a need or need to move the tree whenever it is planted, select a container of size and weight that will take into consideration portability. It is imperative to recall the extra weight that will be added to the container with the dirt, tree, and water. In perpetual positions, bigger, heavier containers might be adequate. A container ought to be as wide as it is tall to give the ideal protection to the roots. On the off chance that you are wanting to show your container tree on a raised deck or gallery, be sure the heaviness of the tree won't bargain the trustworthiness of overhang.

Develop trees that will in general be on the more modest side are commonly most appropriate for a container. On the off chance that the container will be a lasting arrangement, a great many people pick an evergreen that will show well all year. A portion of the well-known evergreen decisions are Hinoki Cypress, Plume Cryptomeria, Italian Cypress, Juniper, Dwarf Spruce, Yew, Little Gem Magnolia, and Bristlecone Pine. This is anything but a total rundown of appropriate evergreen container trees, however surely great spot to begin.

Deciduous trees make superb container examples, however the loss of foliage in the cold weather months is unquestionably a stylish downside for certain zones. Famous decisions for deciduous container trees incorporate Vine Maple, Paperbark Maple, Japanese Maple, Serviceberry, Chinese Redbud, Dogwood, Crepe Myrtle, Magnolia, Weeping Cherry, Staghorn Sumac, and Stewartia.

Evergreen shrubs are likewise magnificent container

plants that can be pruned as trees. A few models incorporate; Boxwood, Holly, Privet, Lilac, Viburnam, Rose-Of-Sharon, Arborvitae, and Witch-hazel.

Legitimate choice in addition to sufficient care and consideration will yield an awesome container tree that will end up being a lovely installation of your open-air space. For the best determination and definite exhortation on container trees, it is highly prescribed to discover a tree master in your general vicinity. Their insight, experience, and choice of value examples far surpasses that of most enormous box retail garden focuses.

CONTAINER GARDENING TIPS

In some cases, there simply is not sufficient yard space to give your green thumb the exercise it desires. Possibly you live in a loft or perhaps your garden is full you actually need to plant more. On the off chance that you have open porch space, at that point fill it with lavish foliage utilizing container gardening.

It bodes well to put resources into quality high terminated artistic pots for your container garden as these do not assimilate water and break in winter. Elective - the new fiberglass and plastic pots can function admirably on the off chance that you picked high quality. These can be extremely light and intense and keep going for quite a long time.

More modest pots limit root development and give little dampness hold, make certain to coordinate container size to your plants at that point go up a size or two, recollect that plant will become bigger soon. Plan for size increment and be in front of the issue numerous beginner containers gardeners face.

Seepage is significant. Waste openings should be 1/2 inch or better in size. Utilizing screen and a rock layer at the lower part of your pot to forestall losing soil and improving seepage is consistently a smart thought. Some utilization coarse plastic screen intended for lakes. Bonsai pot screen additionally functions admirably. Picked window screen last as openings are little and it stops up without any problem.

Containers with lighter tones are ideal on the off chance that you live in hotter customers and your containers will be in direct sun. Lighter tones diminish the measure of warmth ingestion. Roots can reach more than 100 degrees in direct sun with the outcome being helpless development, quickened dry out and dead plants.

Spot your containers up on blocks, wood strips or tiles. There are additionally wheeled stands accessible. This gives bugs no spot to stow away and improves seepage.

Plants that become taller, bigger and spread out require a wide base for equilibrium and steadiness in wind. Plan ahead remembering this while picking a container.

The dirt blend you use is significant. Utilize high quality fertilized soil and avoid ordinary garden soil. Thick style blend keeps the dirt free and very much depleted yet can lessen water holding limit requiring water all the more frequently.

Try not to put un-treated the soil wood contributes your

container soil, they filter nitrogen as they debase and stunt plan development through decrease of nitrogen accessible to your plants.

A fine root structure is greatly improved appropriate for long haul container development. Models, the Japanese Maple, a plant with extremely fine roots, Oak tree - a plant with coarse roots and generally a long tap root. One improves in containers then the other. In the event that you are given and decided, you can develop most any plant in a container.

Make a point to check your plants every day for enough dampness. Container plants should be watered and checked each day.

Get one of those water meter tests and use it for your containers and house plants.

Utilize a water-dissolvable compost at regular intervals to save the dirt nutrient-rich for your plants. Elective - slow delivery pellets useful for a half year of fertilizing with one application.

CHAPTER - 6
LANDSCAPING TREES

Trees are a significant piece of landscaping. While flourishing they make a wonderful commitment to the garden. Adding trees to your landscape, regardless of whether it is one example tree or a gathering of a specific assortment, will extraordinarily improve the appearance and value of your property. Trees can make obscure spots ideal for a seat or table.

They can obstruct winds and add protection. Contingent upon the assortment they can likewise add tone and interest to your yard. Consider whether you need an evergreen, deciduous or blossoming tree.

Picking the correct tree is essential. You should consider numerous variables while choosing a tree and choosing where to plant it. Among them are knowing its develop size and whether it will drop trash. One of the greatest landscaping botches is ill-advised tree arrangement. For instance, a tree with surface roots can pulverize clearing, while a tree that becomes taller than anticipated can meddle with electrical cables or square perspectives.

Start the tree choice cycle by checking out your neighborhood for trees you discover appealing and that have all the earmarks of being progressing admirably. Take photographs of these trees and do explore on them. Consider the regions of your garden that would profit by a tree and select a tree that is fit to this spot. It is a smart thought to recruit a landscape proficient to assist you with choosing trees for your property. They have involvement in many tree types and will have the option to mention to you what will and will not work.

When your trees have been chosen and planted, they should be cared for appropriately. Giving the perfect measure of water is presumably the most vital support concern with regards to trees. Most trees require periodic profound watering, yet acclimate yourself with your tree's particular necessities. Other upkeep contemplations incorporate mulching, fertilizing and pruning.

TIPS FOR SELECTING LANDSCAPING TREES

Indeed, an all-around arranged landscape can increase the value of a home. What is more, with regards to arranging one's landscape, there are various types of trees from which to pick. While an enormous determination can absolutely give the land owner a favorable position, it is likewise conceivable that it might, now and again, additionally make choice of the correct tree an overwhelming and overpowering undertaking. Anyway, what are some essential contemplations for choosing the landscaping trees for one's property?

When choosing trees for your property, it is imperative to initially think about the size of the tree at development. Numerous trees might be very attractive while they are little and growing in containers in the nursery. This underlying allure might be enhanced for those trees that may have wonderful blossoms. However, what measurements should be foreseen when the tree is completely developed? Is it an animal variety known to be little or huge? Now and again property holders neglect to consider what the drawn-out development suggestions might be for the trees they select. Continuously be sure to consider this significant factor when choosing trees for your property.

It is similarly critical to think about the general size of the property. In the event that the property is huge, choosing trees that are too little may not help accomplish any ideal stylish impact the mortgage holder would like to achieve with the landscaping. The trees may seem, by all accounts, to be dispersed excessively rare. An improperly chosen tree planted in some unacceptable area might devalue the property. Unexpectedly, if the property is little, choosing at least one trees that develop to huge measurements at development may swarm the property (or that of a neighbor, best case scenario, or may cause basic harm even from a pessimistic standpoint. Enormous trees that develop on little properties can possibly influence establishments, septic frameworks, housetops, security wall, and the sky is the limit from there.

When choosing trees for one's landscape, a land owner ought to likewise consider the purpose(s) of the tree. Is the expansion of a tree simply stylish? Is it simply utilitarian? Is it a blend? Certain trees loan themselves to explicit purposes, and this may enable the mortgage holder to decide the best tree for their property. For example, if the tree is carefully for beautification, a mortgage holder may choose a tree that presents delightful blossoms, for example, a dogwood or a crabapple, consistently. Maybe the mortgage holder might want a tree that fills a practical need, for example, an enormous oak planted deliberately to either conceal the home during the blistering late spring months or to obstruct the unforgiving winter winds. Maybe the mortgage holder might want a tree that is both tastefully satisfying and useful, for example, planting a maple to protect the home and give delightful fall foliage, or an evergreen that additionally gives some way of haven to the home and gives excellent shading to the property during the regularly distressing cold weather months when deciduous trees have lost their once-vivid leaves.

These are only a couple interesting points when choosing landscaping trees. There might be different contemplations fundamental for a property holder to make. These may incorporate normal temperatures, precipitation, and soil conditions explicit to the territory of the nation in which a mortgage holder lives.

LANDSCAPE TREES – BEST VARIETIES TO GROW

1. **Maples Acer** - Acer signifies "sharp" which depict the focuses on the maple leaves.

2. **Birch Betula** - This shrub develops to 1-1.2 m high. Its bark is non-stripping. It is a sparkly red-copper in shading. It has round leaves that are 6-20 mm measurement.

3. **Cedar Cedrus** - Are trees up to 30-40 m. Now and again they are 60 m tall. They have hot resinous scented wood. They are thick furrowed or may have a square-broke bark.

They are very expansive. Redbud Cercis can. Typically develops to 20-30 feet tall with a 25-35-foot spread. It is generally somewhat short, and commonly has a contorted trunk alongside spreading branches.

4. **Dogwood Cornus** - Their blossoms are little and unnoticeable. They have four greenish-yellow petals that are 4 mm long.

5. **Beech Fagus** - The fruit is little. They have forcefully three-calculated nuts that are consumable yet are unpleasant.

6. **Ginkgo/Maidenhair Ginkgo biloba** - These are enormous trees. They normally arrive at a stature of 66-115 feet. Some in China are much more than 164 feet. The tree has a crown that is precise. They have long branches, normally profound established. They are impervious to wind and snow harm. The more youthful trees are thin and inadequately extended.

The crown will get more extensive as the tree ages. Throughout the fall season, the leaves turn a splendid yellow.

7. **Juniper Juniperus** - These fluctuate fit as a fiddle from tall trees. They are evergreen and have needle-like leaves. Their "berries" are red-earthy colored or orange. Most are blue and are sweet-smelling. They can even be utilized as a flavor.

8. **Dark Gum/Tupelo** - They produce a light, mellow tasting nectar. They can be very costly on account of their heavenly flavor.

9. **Nyssa sylvatica leaf** - Turns purple in the fall season, at that point turns into an extreme splendid red. The bloom is little. The fruit is a dark blue.

10. **Spruce Picea Spruces** - These trees are extremely enormous. They can be 66 to 200 feet in stature once they develop. Their needles or leaves are joined to the branches in a twisting manner.

An incredible spot to look for wonderful trees and shrubs can be at a nursery, garden focus or landscape focus.

ADVANTAGES OF LANDSCAPING TREES

Trees assume a huge function in our current circumstance. This message has been highly promoted by ecological extremist gatherings for over 10 years now, and its ubiquity keeps on growing, as does the gathering of the individuals who credit to its important message. Be that as it may, trees need not exclusively be a country treasure. There are huge advantages to fusing a remarkable tree populace into metropolitan zones, as well. Consequently, numerous mortgage holders, network organizations, and districts put aside a bit of their yearly spending plan to make and look after landscaping. Also, as this training has developed, advantages of doing so have been examined and uncovered.

From a reasonable stance, landscaping trees advantage the normal property holder in a few different ways. Trees planted on the eastern and western sides of homes shade and cool throughout the mid-year and give a windbreak, keeping the home warm throughout the colder time of year. This may decrease a property holder's warming and cooling bill significantly. Fittingly positioned landscaping trees are a fantastic method for atmosphere control on private property. Given adequate space, mortgage holders may decide to develop their own natural food by planting fruit-bearing trees or shrubs. Also, should they decide to sell their home eventually, a mortgage holder may locate that all around planted, very much continued landscaping trees may expand the general value of the property by as much as 15%.

Inside neighborhood networks, the advantages proceed. For example, landscaping trees adjusting concrete give a cooling impact by lessening the measure of warmth ready to be consumed by the solid, just as other framework. This is known as the "heat island impact," and it very well may be fundamentally diminished by earth sound estimates which regions can without much of a stretch oblige in their financial plans. Notwithstanding cooling the network everywhere, trees that adjust public walkways and other cleared surfaces give a layer of assurance against the components that may broaden the life of the cleared surface. The less cash required for this way of upkeep implies greater accessibility of assets for different undertakings or needs, or the preservation of citizen dollars. Like those planted on close to home property, deliberately planted landscaping trees likewise give a proportion of atmosphere control for network organizations, associations, or neighborhood government structures. They additionally give protection and decrease glare.

Maybe generally fascinating, research shows that streets adjusted by trees advance wellbeing in view of the observation by drivers of smaller streets. This is valid, as well, of intently separated trees adjusting streets, which cause drivers to see over the top speed and, thusly, slow down. Trees additionally advance wellbeing by making a boundary among drivers and walkers.

Ecological advantages of landscaping trees inside metropolitan and rural regions incorporate a characteristic decrease of carbon dioxide, just as assimilation of other natural toxins. Trees lessen disintegration, just as control flooding by breaking precipitation and water seepage ways. Blossoming trees give food to natural life. Also, clamor contamination is reduced via landscaping trees.

Studies demonstrate that sociological advantages of landscaping trees in metropolitan and rural regions incorporate making a sentiment of unwinding for spectators, while different examinations show that patients in medical clinic rooms whose view incorporates trees commonly recuperate quicker than patients whose rooms do exclude such view.

There are various motivations to plant and keep up the same number of trees as are conceivable and viable inside some random populated, metropolitan territory. The advantages are very extensive and fulfilling.

CHAPTER - 7
FRUITS TREES

HOW TO GROW FRUIT TREES

Planting fruit trees is anything but a troublesome undertaking, yet there are a couple of contemplations you should make before you make the strides vital for planting fruit trees in the ground. Such things as what zone you live in and where in your property to put your trees are significant. Placing a tree in the ground is simple, however your prosperity or disappointment can happen by picking some unacceptable tree or placing it in some unacceptable spot.

Fruit trees are a great alternative for your garden. It not just gives you better harvest all during that time yet in addition adds decorative component to your garden through giving spring season blossoms, sensitive smell and summer shadow. Fruit trees are generally simple to develop and sensible with less exertion. You can develop alluring trees and exposed abundance of fruits to eat, prepare, safeguard and additionally sell. Yet, how you can get these advantages? Here are some straightforward rules on the best way to develop incredible fruit trees and make the most of its advantages.

Planting - For planting fruit trees, you should go for open bright spot shielded from solid breeze. They can be filled in expansive scope of soil and need great waste.

Trees like pears, plums and other bear heavier soils. This help improves soil extravagance. Winter is the best season for fruit trees plantation. Planting fruit trees are ordinary same as other tree plantation which incorporates burrowing soil to filling fertilizer and setting the seeds. You have to deal with the water gracefully, do not overwater or submerged the plant. Evade roots to be left dry and make a point to plunge the established trees in water. You can decide on natural and aquaculture technique for your garden.

Caring - You should utilize a decent adjusted manure at the hour of late-winter and harvest time. Sprinkle the compost under the tree's limbs. You can likewise utilize moderate delivery manure at planting time. Watering is a fundamental need of any new trees, for example, decorative trees or fruit trees, in dry periods utilize customary watering or give profound soakings in summer. You can utilize natural manure, for example, Mulch, this assists with saving the dampness and ensure nutrients and roots. This forestalls the development of grass and weeds.

Pruning and Training - Pruning is significant and this empowers resurrection of fruiting wood that produce quality fruit. This lets light go into the tree and helps eliminates unfortunate parts and managing additionally deal with a tree's tallness. During the essential phase of development, the fundamental point is to build up the figure and systems that underpins substantial fruit crops. Pruning ought to be done while the trees are resting and ensure your gardening apparatuses like scissors, secateurs are pointed and cut the undesirable development bud without any problem. While eliminating the dead or undesirable wood, you should consistently slice or eliminate through the solid bud beneath the polluted area.

Make huge slices to get secured against bothers.

Diseases - Most infections are spread in fruit trees are through wind, sticky climate and dampness. Guarantee that you consume all fallen defiled leaves or spoiled fruits.

The fruit trees should be kept in refresh and circulated air through position and trim the middle part for appropriate air development. You can utilize copper splash that forestalls infection assaulting leaves, fruits and stems. However, be minimal careful prior to utilizing copper shower as it can harm your fruit leaves.

RESOURCES

Uncovered root fruit brambles and trees speak to an ideal answer for anybody with a drawn-out interest in setting up their own smaller than normal plantation without investing a great deal of energy in tending individual trees.

Accessible from business providers requiring little to no effort, these trees can be planted in gardens and in porch fruit pots, and can create numerous sorts of produce each year.

Savvy and ready to face long stretches of utilization, a fruit tree will more than make up its value after some time.

SCOPE OF FRUIT

Most fruit trees available to be purchased produce a wide scope of pre-fall and early harvest time blooming fruit. Exposed root trees with numerous branches are especially appropriate to growing Braeburn, Bramley, Cox, and Valentine apples, which can be picked in the pre-winter, and can be eaten off the branch or cooked into pies.

Similar qualities can be found in exposed root pear trees, which will in general create hefty yields from a self-fruitful base.

More extraordinary uncovered root trees highlighting peaches, apricots, and nectarines can likewise be effortlessly filled in the United Kingdom, and regularly advantage from an early bloom in pre-fall. Similarly, cherry and Victoria plum trees with a late bloom will give extraordinary harvests after some time.

The distinction in taste and newness from monetarily purchased fruit will be huge, while the overall harvests the trees produce can convert into significant benefits when sold.

SIMPLE AND LOW COST

A small-scale plantation can be made at almost no expense and will require a restricted measure of upkeep. The trees themselves can be bought from cold stockpiling and either filled in soil, or inside pots intended to help smaller than expected fruit trees.

The last are exceptionally designed from bantam stock, which confines all out-stature development to around 7 feet. Most kinds of fruit trees available to be purchased are likewise self-pollinating, and will require small watering.

While some cherry fruit trees may require more considerable degrees of shade, most exposed root fruit trees can be just developed as a feature of yard fruit pots in little gardens.

DURABLE VALUE

Maybe the main advantage of possessing exposed fruit trees is their value for cash throughout an extensive stretch of time.

The primary year may not generally produce a predictable yield; however, persistence and infrequent support will imply that a solid fruit tree plantation can create guard crops for thirty to forty years once the trees arrive at their greatest statures.

CHAPTER - 8
NUT TREES

Nut trees give us definitely more than heavenly, highly nutritious nuts. Numerous varieties make for superb shade trees, and have highly appealing structures, foliage, bark and different highlights, making them ideal for the property landscape.

The short meaning of a nut is any hard-shell dry fruit or seed that contains at least one palatable bit. The organic significance is somewhat more detailed, yet for our motivations, let the regular term do the trick. To explain things further, a peanut, organically, is not a nut by any means, yet rather the fruit and seed of a vegetable.

FOR ITS STRENGTH

Nuts are a nutritionally thick food. They are an extraordinary wellspring of protein, iron, calcium, different minerals, fundamental amino acids, and B nutrients, and contain no cholesterol. They are perhaps the most extravagant wellspring of nutrient E, and the fats found in nuts are heart solid. Chestnuts are the main nut with any nutrient C, made for the most part out of sugars and minerals, and low in fat and calories.

PUTTING DOWN ROOTS

Most nut trees are moderately simple to develop and deal with. Generally, buying joined trees for transplanting is simpler than beginning from seed. Seedlings from nuts may have slight varieties from the parent tree and could take more time to set up and bear nuts. Remember that dissimilar to fruit trees, which are regularly united onto size-controlling rootstocks, most nut trees are joined onto set up foundations of the equivalent or related species. These unions are basically clones of a known parent or cultivar. Since these roots have just developed for a year or somewhere in the vicinity, your hang tight for the primary nut gather is abbreviated extensively. Named cultivars or varieties are best regarding toughness, illness obstruction, and production of enormous, substantial nuts that are frequently simpler to separate open.

Most nut trees require at least two trees for fertilization and nut production, and they frequently incline toward profound, all around depleted soil and full sun. A few animal varieties have long taproots, so in the event that you are transplanting nut trees with root balls or exposed roots, it is prescribed to burrow a genuinely profound opening at planting time to limit any harm and oblige the roots. Natural issue blended into the dirt is gainful, especially for walnuts and related species. Numerous trees will eventually become very enormous, so abundant space between them is significant, yet close to 100 feet separated to help with fertilization. Check the tallness and spread of your cultivars to decide a decent separation.

Growing nut trees requires persistence. At the point when

a nut crop is at last created, leave it to develop on the tree. The nuts will normally fall, and can undoubtedly be accumulated off the ground. You can likewise spread a canvas under the tree and shake the nuts free when they are developed.

BEST NUT TREES VARIETIES TO GROW

On the off chance that you intend to plant trees on your pastime ranches, think about these different sorts of nuts, including almonds, walnuts and pine nuts.

Wood trees put their energy into growing up to the shelter. Plantation trees, then again, chose to be short and spreading, placed their energy into the production of nuts. Here is a testing of nut varieties and their attributes to assist you with picking the correct nut trees to develop on your homestead.

1. Almond

Almonds are regularly perceived for their beautiful spring blossom. They are one of the principal trees to sprout in our melting away winter meaning a turn in the season has arrived. Almonds lean toward a parched atmosphere. Spring downpours and cold evenings are a test for a blossoming almond. Regularly our clients appreciate them just for their appealing development propensity and sprout. Reap your almonds when in any event 75% of the fruits have aired out to uncover the seed inside.

They should have two cultivars for cross-fertilization and are pollinated by honey bees.

2. Hazelnut

Hazelnut (Filbert) develop around 12-feet high and spreading up to 16 ft. They are moderately little and simple to oversee. Fortunately, the nuts promptly tumble off the tree, no stepping stools or uncommon gear is essential for reap. The trees produce sweet nuts in the pre-fall and into fall. We start to see fruit in 3-5 years. They do require two unique varieties for cross fertilization which is wind driven so closeness is significant.

3. Walnuts

Walnuts are a standout amongst other plant wellsprings of protein. They are plentiful in fiber, B nutrients, magnesium, and cell reinforcements, for example, Vitamin E. They are likewise higher than generally nuts in omega-3 basic unsaturated fats. They are delightful as a tidbit, prepared in servings of mixed greens and oats/oats, even joined into pesto sauce. We are offering two generally little assortment/rootstock blends.

They are self-pollinating, however nuts from cross-pollinated trees might be of higher quality.

4. Chestnut (Castanea sp.)

Before chestnut scourge almost cleared out the North American chestnut (C. dentata), it included a fourth of all trees in the Carolinian backwoods of North America through the Appalachian Mountains and into Canada.

Today, plant researchers are endeavoring to bring chestnut trees back from the verge, backcrossing the

North American species and curse safe Asian species, for example, Chinese and Japanese chestnuts (C. mollissima and C. crenata, separately)— the two of which likewise fill in the U.S. Contingent upon which of the huge number of cultivars are planted, chestnuts will fill in districts as far north as Michigan, Wisconsin and Canada and as far south as Georgia and northern Florida.

Contingent upon the assortment, chestnuts grow 40 to 80 feet wide and high, however the size of this new assortment a work in progress is not yet known.

A chestnut plantation will require less interest in splashing for bothers than, state, apples or peaches."

The genuine constraint is soil type and sufficient dampness.

5. Hickory (Carya sp.)

The shagbark hickory (C. ovata) and shellbark (C. laciniosa) hickory are eastern North America locals, going from southern Canada to northern Mexico. They are moderate growing trees that may take a very long time to tolerate nuts yet can live for quite a long time. Joined hickory varieties may yield more solid yet not quicker nut production.

Hickory trees need a long taproot before they can start delivering nuts.

Hickories are freezing strong, adjust well to upset territories and endure helpless soils. They produce little, sweet nuts inside incredibly solid shells. The trees develop to around 60 feet tall. You need to plant two varieties whose blossoming and dust shedding suit each other's fertilization timing.

6. (Macadamia integrifolia)

The macadamia, acquainted with Hawaii from Australia in the late nineteenth century, can likewise develop and create well in little areas of southwestern California and southern Florida

7. Pine Nut (Pinus edulis)

Evergreen pinons or pinions, local to western states, produce pieces in their pinecones. Contingent upon the species and growing conditions, pine nut trees might be huge or little, quick or moderate growing, heat-lenient or cold-solid, and produce a couple or up to 200 parts for each cone.

8. Pistachio (Pistacia sp.)

The moderate growing pistachio flourishes in locales with short, cool winters followed by blistering, dry summers. Dry spell lenient, the tree fills well in bone-dry sandy-dirtied districts of the American Southwest with a lot of sun, where there are no ices to execute its spring blossoms.

CHAPTER - 9
VALUE - ADDED TREES (BONSAI)

The bonsai business is blasting, as an ever-increasing number of individuals become authorities of these brilliant minuscule trees. Bonsai trees permit city inhabitants, who have restricted yard space, or even no yard by any means, to appreciate the excellence of trees in their homes. A bonsai business is ideal for little producers with restricted space, as bonsai trees take up almost no territory, and can create significant benefits. A few cultivators have practical experience in starter plants that are prepared to prepare, while others want to sell prepared plants, as the benefits are higher. For bonsai cultivators with tolerance, adult "example" trees can bring many dollars from genuine bonsai gatherers. The web has made significantly more premium in bonsai, and furthermore gives another commercial center to cultivators to sell their bonsai plants to a lot more extensive crowd.

A bonsai tree is a little tree that is planted inside a container. Truth be told, the expression "bonsai" in a real sense signifies "planted in a container" in Japanese.

Bonsai alludes to the specialty of developing these little trees and is an indispensable portion of Japanese culture going back to the mid fourteenth century. Once delighted in by just the wealthiest blue-bloods and high-positioning individuals from Japanese society, bonsai is presently a work of art that is appreciated by individuals from all around the globe.

To decide the best area to show your bonsai, you should comprehend what sort of tree it is and whether it is an indoor or outside plant.

Most basic sorts of bonsai, for example, juniper, pine and tidy trees are open air plants and ought to be presented to the seasons like their bigger partners. Open air bonsai likewise incorporate deciduous trees, implying that their leaves change with the seasons. These incorporate maple, elms and gingko.

Indoor bonsai trees are normally subtropical species which flourish off of stable temperatures consistently. These incorporate jade plants, Hawaiian umbrella trees, and ficus trees.

Whenever you have sorted out what kind of bonsai tree you have, the rest is genuinely basic. Here are some broad tips on bonsai tree situating that ordinarily apply to a wide range of bonsai trees.

Situating - Your bonsai ought to be avoided direct warmth or draft.

Lighting - Keep your bonsai in region with a lot of daylight.

Humidity - Bonsais need mugginess or humidity to keep their dirt wet.

APPROACHES TO GROW BONSAI PROFITABLY

Bonsai seed germination is the official term for the compelling artwork of duplicating your bonsai plant. It is the place where, as most plants, seeds sprout after a brief time of being torpid or stale. A ton of components impact the elements of sprouting bonsai seeds. This incorporates, yet is not restricted to: time, water, temperature, oxygen and light. As a bonsai proprietor, you should know the essentialness of every one of these components to make your bonsai seed germination as beneficial and productive as could reasonably be expected.

Bonsai seed germination requires tolerance on your part. Seed does not fill for the time being in any plant, and your bonsai is no special case. You should give a broad measure of time before you genuinely receive the rewards of planting for your bonsai's augmentation. The entire thing is a craftsmanship itself of which you are perhaps the greatest patron. It might require some investment and exertion, however when you see your bonsai plant develop, you will clearly observe that it merits all your time and exertion.

One significant actuality to consider is that you cannot develop a dozing seed. A dozing seed is in the phase of torpidity. Basically, you have to wake it to transform it.

The cycle of cold separation is accomplished for this very reason. A sandwich sack might be adequate for your seed or some other shut container with comparable highlights.

Soak vermiculite and spot, it clinched. For each and every seed, there must be in any event ten units of vermiculite. To forestall pervasion of parasites, you may likewise need to add different fixings, for example, compound arrangements which are promptly accessible for plant lovers like you. Eighty or ninety days in the fridge generally does the secret to stir the seeds. Doing them by mass spares time and you will not stress over having undermined quality however long you have enough vermiculite to back it up.

There is one general method of growing bonsai, and since it is an extraordinary plant, you have to accept additional care as you do it. Absorb the seeds tepid water for around two hours prior to planting it. At that point you can put it in a pot around 7 centimeters down or more profound on the off chance that you are to develop it outside. The point of doing this is to have the bonsai seedling flourish.

It is imperative to take note of that when the seedlings have their foundations on the dirt where you have planted them, you have to put it in its containers. Notice legitimate planning and do not do this on a colder time of year. Discover a period where you can do it in spring or summer. Before you move the plant, you have to water it initial a couple of hours prior. Build-up it in a sheltered and obscure territory for a large portion of a month with a constant flow of light and dampness.

WHAT IS A SHRUB?

Shrubs are woody plants that have a few fundamental stems. They can be either deciduous (go lethargic and drop their leaves in winter) or evergreen (don't go torpid and keep their leaves through winter).

THE BASICS

Zone - Make sure the shrub you are planting is viable with your growing zone. On the off chance that you are growing a shrub in a container, it is a smart thought to get one that is cold solid to one zone lower on the grounds that the roots have less protection than if they were in the ground.

Presentation - Know the area you are planting in and pick likewise. Shrubs marked full sun need at any rate 6 hours of direct daylight every day, those named part shade ought to get 4 to 6 hours, and ones named full shade should just get a couple of long stretches of morning sun. Try not to swindle blossoming shrubs out of their sun, they will not bloom too.

Soil - Most shrubs are genuinely versatile to wide scope of soil as long as it depletes well.

PLANTING SHRUBS

When to plant shrubs: Shrubs can be planted practically any season, in spite of the fact that spring and fall are regularly the best occasions to plant.

Warm atmospheres - Plant early enough in spring so attaches have sufficient opportunity to change before temperatures rise. In the case of planting in summer, or if a rebel heat wave hits, be extra mindful about watering recently planted shrubs. Planting in fall permits shrubs time to get ready for a spring development spray.

Cold atmospheres - Plant in spring once the ground defrosts and temperatures begin to heat up. Water industriously whenever planted in summer; and in the fall, plant sufficiently early so they can get comfortable before the ground freezes.

The most effective method to plant shrubs - Dig an opening about double the width and similarly as profound as the size of the container. Carefully eliminate the plant from the pot and release the roots with your fingers. Spot the plant in the opening and refill with the local soil that was eliminated, firming the dirt into place as you go. The highest point of the root ball ought to be covered by about ½" of soil when wrapped up. Cover with a 2-3" layer of destroyed bark mulch.

PREPARING SHRUB TREES - ESPALIER AND PLEACHING

Pleaching - is a strategy for preparing trees to create a tight screen or fence by tying in and entwining adaptable youthful shoots along a supporting system. Utilize this procedure to make strolls, arbors, passages and curves.

Continuously select youthful, whippy plants that are all the more effectively prepared for pleaching. Plant in winter and during early years likewise prune in the colder time of year when plants are leafless and torpid. Train and tie new shoots in over the late spring. Once pleached trees have arrived at their full degree, prune in the mid-year, pruning to shape the tree development and lessen its force.

Espalier - Espaliers prepared into level two-dimensional structures, are ideal, for decorative purposes, yet in addition for gardens in which space is restricted. In a mild atmosphere, they might be planted close to a divider that can reflect more daylight and hold heat for the time being or planted so they assimilate most extreme daylight via preparing them corresponding to the equator.

Pleaching and espalier are tree-molding strategies in which trees are prepared to develop along a level plane. Advocated by the Romans and seventeenth century French and Italian arborists, these procedures have suffered and now carry magnificence and capacity to our cutting-edge landscapes.

Pleaching and espalier are both tree-molding procedures that contribute shrewd, unmistakable looks to a landscape or garden.

PLEACHING - INTERTWINING BRANCHES

French and Italian landscapers in the seventeenth and eighteenth hundred of years set up the method of pleaching. This type of forming trees ordinarily includes a line of trees with lower expands all pruned and upper branches interweaved. Intertwined branches inevitably become together and make a strong raised support over uncovered trunks.

Pleaching is additionally the method that can make an all-encompassing opening of trees, where once more, trunks are kept exposed up to a specific tallness, and all branches above are joined. In an opening there will be two equal columns of trees with upper branches interlocking and interlacing to shape an angled roof.

Lime trees are customarily utilized for pleaching, however crab apples and photinia are currently very basic also.

HOW TO PLEACH TREES

Start with trees that have ramrod-straight trunks and are of reliable circumference. Plant trees with long, solid stakes in any event 8 feet separated. Use bamboo shafts or wire links to make the structure along which branches will be prepared. Twist youthful shoots and bind to the system. Cut back shoots that don't twist effectively or that are growing the incorrect way. As branches develop and work, they will require normal pruning.

ESPALIER - TRAINED INTO A PATTERN

The act of espalier–preparing trees to fill in a particular example along a level plane—has been around for a very long time. It was the Romans who presented this growing procedure wherein trees develop along level backings, for example, dividers or wall.

These days instances of this growing procedure can be found openly gardens, on huge bequests (think the Biltmore in South Carolina), and even at amusement parks. It can likewise be effectively consolidated into a mortgage holder's landscaping whether the property is little or enormous.

Espalier trees are wonderful and useful. Their examples can be casual (following their normal shape) or formal, as in a stepping stool build, or upward inclining branches equitably dispersed separated, or in U-molded varieties.

An advantage of espalier trees on a little property is the utilizing of space. A plantation of fruit trees can develop along a limit divider or fence without taking up a lot of grounds. The open idea of development implies that practically all fruit on the trees gets a lot of sun.

In Florida, great fruit trees to espalier incorporate citrus, loquat, and Natal plum. (Note, however, that lone the loquat will normally fit a conventional development design; the others favor a casual example.)

STEP BY STEP INSTRUCTIONS TO ESPALIER TREES

A solitary espaliered tree needs at any rate 8 straight feet and an area in full sun. Utilize a current help (divider or fence) or an unattached system. Set posts or stakes 16 inches separated and stretch three or four lines of equal wires across them. Plant tree 6-8 crawls out from the wires. Twist existing branches in your picked example and secure to wires with plant ties. Prune off undesirable branches. Slice focus trunk to simply above first wire, leaving buds underneath cut. As buds form into branches, train them along your example.

SOME PLEACHED AND ESPALIER TREES

1. Acer campestre/Field Maple

Acer campestre is a medium-sized deciduous tree, accessible here on a pleached outline. The leaves of this local field maple turn brilliant yellow in the pre-winter. This example makes a fine pleached tree. Similarly, as with a large number of the local trees, it is an extreme competitor and will endure dry spell, air contamination and soil compaction.

2.Carpinus betulus/Hornbeam

Because of Hornbeam's capacity to recover in the wake of pruning, this famous deciduous tree is ideal for shaping espalier or pleached trees. It has an extremely reduced and shut crown with a carefully vertical trunk with smooth dim dark bark. The leaves are a new green tone in spring and turn brilliant yellow in the harvest time. Carpinus betulus is tough and can be planted in sun or conceal and in all dirt sorts.

3. Fagus sylvatica/Beech

Fagus sylvatica is mainstream deciduous tree for pleaching because of its capacity to hold its leaves all through the cold weather months. Bark is smooth gleaming dim and the leaves are new green turning an awesome yellow-orange in the harvest time. Beech lean towards nutritious, very much depleted soils, it is delicate to salt and soil contamination, everything being equal. Can be planted in sun or shade.

4. Malus 'Red Sentinel'/Flowering Crab Apple

Malus are little deciduous crab apple trees with outward growing branches. The green leaves arise bronze hued and have red-colored stems. They can offer abundant bloom in the spring, trailed by fruist that can stay on the tree all through the pre-winter.

Varieties incorporate Red Sentinel Malus evereste and John Downie

Genuinely solid, these pretty little trees will fill in sandy, mud or calcareous soils in sun to light shade.

5. Tilia platyphyllos/Broad-leaved Lime

Tilia platyphyllos is a quickly developing Broad-Leaved Lime tree which has delectable heart-molded foliage which gives the tree a sound appearance lasting through the year; the leaves have a lime yellow pre-winter. This intense tree is fit for enduring metropolitan conditions and reacts well to normal pruning. It will endure most soil types, including earth soils.

6. Tilia x europaea 'Pallida'/Common Lime

Tilia europaea is a deciduous tree with a straight, vertical stem and can be filled in a wide range of soil. The leaves are skewed heart-molded, glossy dim green with a light green underside turning brilliant yellow in fall.

This assortment comes into leaf right off the bat in spring and loses its leaves from the get-go in fall.

7. Prunus laurocerasus/Cherry Laurel

Prunus laurocerasus is a famous tree, with an upstanding and shaggy propensity which is amazing all year screening in its pleached structure. Its enormous leaves are curved, sparkly and brilliant green and have little, sweet-smelling, white blossoms, which fill in vertical racemes, trailed by little, cherry-like fruit. Prunus laurocerasus Novita likewise makes a fine pleached cherry shrub.

8. Magnolia grandiflora

Magnolia grandiflora is an exemplary elaborate evergreen with huge polished green leaves with a coppery, nearly textured underside. The wonderful, enormous, sweet-smelling white blossoms show up in pre-fall through to harvest time. Magnolia grandiflora fits being pleached, which does not influence production of their blossoms and is subsequently an extraordinary decision for screening over a fence line.

CHAPTER - 10
HIGH - VALUE TREES PRODUCTS

In the event that you own a couple of sections of land, think about turning into a tree rancher. It is earth-accommodating and more productive than you may envision when you develop high-value trees.

Conventional tree ranches are a lot of like a plantation with one essential harvest, saw and mash logs. In the South, most tree ranchers develop loblolly pines, in the Northwest, douglas fir and somewhere else an assortment of evergreen and deciduous trees developed fundamentally for mash and timber.

To succeed and benefit as a tree rancher today, it is critical to move from product trees that take a very long time to develop and pay close to nothing, to planting, growing and collecting 'specialty' trees that can deliver more pay quicker. You need trees that are:

Simple to develop – Choose trees that can be planted with low direct expenses and low support and collect expenses. In many occurrences, that implies local trees, the species that fill normally in your district.

Quickly developing – A remain of Douglas fir, for instance, takes around 50 years to develop to wood reap size, while a remain of similar animal categories, developed for Christmas trees can be prepared for collect in 7-8 years. This implies growing Christmas trees makes a tree rancher around multiple times more benefit per section of land. There are other quickly developing trees that can deliver a customary pay from limbs, shoots, sap, cones, fruit or nuts.

Produce high-value products – The correct trees can deliver a wealth of usable things, for example, craft fibers, decorative wood, food, ornamentals and live plants. While the majority of these high-value products are inconsequential to large corporate tree ranchers, they can carry a significant pay to little tree ranchers who have the opportunity and market information to plant, keep up and reap these trees.

Some of these high – value trees are;

Craft fibers – Craft fiber is essentially wood that can be woven. It incorporates the bark, braces, strips and shoots of a tree. These fibers are valued by bushel weavers, and other fiber craftsmen. For instance, supports, produced using the delaminated layers of a tree log, can create as much as $500 worth of product from one little tree. A most loved animal categories for this is the Black debris tree, otherwise called the 'crate tree.'

Another case of a productive craft fiber is willow shoots. Willow trees become pretty much anyplace they can get enough dampness, and are anything but difficult to build up and keep up. Every year, the willow shoots can be pruned, and the following spring, you will have another yield of shoots prepared to gather in the fall. The new willow shoots and catkins are sought after from flower specialists and botanical wholesalers, with a significantly greater interest from crafters who utilize the bars to weave crates and other fiber expressions.

Decorative wood – Decorative wood is sawn wood that is valued for its novel appearance. Burls, figured wood and hued wood are three kinds of decorative wood consistently popular for expressions and crafts, cabinetry, furniture making and instruments. The best part is that decorative wood has no termination date. A reaped log can sit in your shed or horse shelter for quite a long time, and chances are acceptable the value would be expanding every year. One lumber vendor says the cost of decorative wood has expanded 15% every year for as long as 30 years, since it is hard to find.

As indicated by lumber specialists, a section of land planted in huge leaf maple and prepared to create figured wood could be worth $500,000 at development, notwithstanding pay from intermittent diminishing. Other tree species can be similarly significant too. Severe cherry, thought about a weed tree by lumberjacks, produces level groups of bark that is offered to crafters in short strips.

Fruits and nuts – Many trees, for example, walnut, can create fruits and nuts while growing to lumber size. Likewise, current agroforestry rehearses permit growing other fruit crops, similar to berries, as an understory crop with the correct tree dispersing. Ginseng, another high-value crop, can be developed under a shade of trees. Ginseng costs have been about $300 a pound for develop establishes lately.

Ornamentals – Woody ornamentals are trees and shrubs that develop back in the wake of cutting, and are mainstream with flower architects, who use them for rounding out huge flower bundles.

Mainstream woodies incorporate lilac, forsythia and wine tool willow. All are lasting, so whenever they are set up, they require basically no upkeep other than gathering the branches each year.

As should be obvious, growing high-value trees on a tree ranch can carry a lot of higher benefits to producers. Start-up costs are low, and request is growing each year.

Food - People from everywhere the world accumulate nutritional products from trees including fruits, nuts, seeds, leaves, bark and even sap.

Tree products have been a significant piece of diets for a large number of years, from early people gathering fruits and nuts (there is proof of people eating apples in the Neolithic time frame) to the primary development of significant trees, for example, mango (Mangifera indica) which has been filled in India for more than 4,000 years.

Today, products, for example, apples, oranges, pistachios and brazil nuts are regularly eaten the world over and structure the reason for multi-million-dollar ventures –

the apple business is assessed to be worth US $10 billion per year, for instance.

At the neighborhood level, eatable tree products are frequently highly valued by nearby networks as a center piece of their eating routine, as a significant enhancement or to continue them when food is occasionally scant or when harvests are poor. This function as 'crisis' food sources is especially significant and there are a few instances of whole networks enduring times of starvation by gathering food from trees.

Live plants - Live plants and horticulture products incorporate live trees, shrubs and brambles and different merchandise regularly provided by nursery gardeners or flower vendors for planting or decorative use.

Expanding levels of blossom production and development of decorative plants give the EU one of the world's highest densities of bloom production per hectare – 10% of complete world territory and 44% of world blossom and pot-plant production.

The EU is a net exporter of pot plants, conifers and strong enduring plants, bulbs and corms, a net shipper of cut blossoms and cut foliage and has a net exchange surplus for live plants and horticulture products.

RESOURCES

Legitimate bases - The system for live plants and gardening products covers all products falling under part 6 of the joined terminology, and the area itself is covered by the single regular association of the business sectors in farming products EU guideline 1308/2013. The European Commission screens production, market and exchange streams the area.

In the structure of the single basic association of the business sectors in farming products guideline, the European Commission is approved to:

help change flexibly to reflect market necessities by taking measures to improve quality, better sort out production, handling and showcasing, make it simpler to follow market value patterns, and help build up short and long-haul figures dependent on methods for production;

require import licenses for specific products, as an instrument for dealing with their business sectors;

fix yearly (before the promoting season) at least one least cost for fares to non-EU nations of bulbs, tubers, tuberous roots, corms, crowns and rhizomes, torpid (products falling under CN code 0601 10). For this situation, such products must be sent out at a value equivalent to or over the base fixed cost.

CHAPTER - 11
JAPANESE MAPLES

These exquisite trees are consistently popular by property holders and landscapers. It could conceivably be the ideal tree for a little claim to fame tree nursery, as there is interest for both more modest trees for those on a tight spending plan just as bigger "example" trees for those with profound pockets. Additionally, there are many named varieties, in both red and green, and in the two sorts, expansive leaf and cut leaf. The more modest size of most Japanese maples makes them an ideal tree for container growing, so hundreds can be developed available to be purchased in even a little terrace nursery.

The Japanese Maple (Acer palmatum) is an impressive expansion to any garden and will develop from 0.5m to 25m contribution a wonder of shading with its unmistakable molded leaves.

Initially developed in Japan (thus the name), the hitting Japanese Maple with its amazing trunk and pretty leaves (called momiji – which means infant hands) have been famous garden augmentations since the 1800s.

WHEN TO PLANT A JAPANESE MAPLE

As indicated by Eco Organic you can plant Japanese maple whenever of year yet being deciduous it will shed its leaves in winter.

Purchasing a maple in Autumn permits you to see the bright leaves in full brilliance.

GROWING YOUR JAPANESE MAPLE

The conservative root arrangement of the Japanese maple makes it ideal for downtown yards as the roots won't meddle with your home's establishment. It additionally makes them ideal for growing in pots.

Simply be careful that every maple will arrive at an alternate stature. One of the mid-range varieties is Seiryu which can grow up to 4 meters.

BEST VARIETIES TO GROW

- **Japanese maple bonsai**

The Bonsai Society of Australia suggests pruning your Japanese maple in June once the leaves have fallen (which occurs around May to mid-July).

In more smoking pieces of the nation, Japanese maples will fill best to some degree conceal. In cooler atmospheres like Tasmania the maple favors a situation with great light.

The blast of Autumn tone is the thing that makes the Japanese maple so famous. Regardless of whether that is a bonsai or a full-size Acer palmatum, they will arrive at their maximum capacity whenever kept out of the ice and wind.

- **Bantam sobbing maple**

Raraflora on the south shore of NSW unites an assortment of uncommon plants including the trim leaf and dissectum varieties of Japanese maple.

Specialsing in the sobbing maple, they deliver Australia wide and costs start at $75 for a 2-4-year-old tree.

- **Osakasuki**

The leaves of the Osakasuki have an energetic shading and can be pink through to red, directly through to most profound red.

The shading is reliant on the conditions and atmosphere with cooler climes creating the most dynamic shades.

- **Bloodgood maple**

Bloodgood (above) is a developed type of Atropurpureum.

Like most Japanese maples, the Bloodgood is a moderate growing tree growing 30 to 60 centimeters every year.

It will develop to full stature 3-4 meters in around 15 years yet can likewise be developed into a bantam variant known as Shaina.

- **Coral bark maple**

Like most Japanese Maples, the Sango Kaku, otherwise called Coral Bark, develops promptly close by different maples and shrubs.

The Coral Bark develops to a stature of 6-7 meters with a lovely spread that goes from 5-6 meters wide.

Planting Japanese maples close to trees and shrubs with blue, green or purple foliage gives a technicolor vibe that will rejuvenate your garden.

- **Red mythical beast maple**

The Red Dragon maple which started in New Zealand has rich purple-red silky leaves.

The bantam Red Dragon develops to around 60 centimeters though the full-size variant can arrive at just about 2 meters.

JAPANESE MAPLE RESOURCES

The Maple Society's goals are to energize the development of maples, to empower individuals to gain from one another about their propagation, development, presentation and ID, and to encourage the investigation of the plant science, utilizes and social requirements of maples. Articles shared through the Maple Society's Open Science Initiative are accessible at Open Science at the Maple Society | The Maple Society.

Government funded schooling and overall cooperation are at the core of the Maple Society's motivation. The grasp of an Open Science model is a characteristic augmentation of our continuous work through logical symposia, distributed material, gatherings and on line. The Maple Society's Open Science Initiative offers articles identified with maple herbal science and culture - including Peter Gregory's Maple Profiles - in a few dialects. There is likewise a Paper Links page which records logical papers concerning Acer that are openly accessible on the web.

The OSI is accessible to the two individuals and non-individuals from the Maple Society.

In the event that you are an individual from the Maple Society, you are qualified for be perceived as such on your client profile. Snap on your name (upper right on the screen), at that point Personal Details. Enter your genuine name in the line for Maple Society Sign-up. When your participation in the general public is affirmed, a Maple Society flag will show on your profile.

CHAPTER - 12
CHRISTMAS TREES

A Christmas tree is a beautified tree, normally an evergreen conifer, for example, a tidy, pine or fir, or a counterfeit tree of comparative appearance, related with the festival of Christmas, beginning in Northern Europe. The exceptionally was created in archaic Livonia (present-day Estonia and Latvia), and in early current Germany where Protestant Germans brought finished trees into their homes. It procured ubiquity past the Lutheran territories of Germany and the Baltic nations during the second 50% of the nineteenth century, from the outset among the privileged societies. The Catholic Church had since quite a while ago opposed this Protestant custom and the Christmas Tree represented the first run through in Vatican in 1982.

The tree was generally designed with "roses made of shaded paper, apples, wafers, glitter, and sweetmeats". In the eighteenth century, it started to be enlightened by candles, which were eventually supplanted by Christmas lights after the coming of zap. Today, there is a wide assortment of conventional and current trimmings, for example, wreaths, trinkets, glitter, and candy sticks. A heavenly attendant or star may be set at the highest point of the tree to speak to the Angel Gabriel or the Star of Bethlehem, separately, from the Nativity. Palatable things, for example, gingerbread, chocolate and different desserts are likewise well known and are attached to or dangled from the tree's limbs with strips.

In the Western Christian convention, Christmas trees are differently raised on days, for example, the principal day of Advent or even as late as Christmas Eve relying upon the nation; customs of a similar confidence hold that the two customary days when Christmas enhancements, for example, the Christmas tree, are eliminated are Twelfth Night and, on the off chance that they are not brought down on that day, Candlemas, the last of which closes the Christmas-Epiphany season in certain sections.

SOIL FERTILITY REQUIREMENTS FOR CHRISTMAS TREES

At the point when plantations are set up on rich soil and appropriately oversaw, Christmas tree production can be a beneficial business.

Christmas trees can be effectively developed on an assortment of soil types, yet all around depleted, loamy soils are best for Christmas tree production. Careful administration of soil richness can improve tree quality and appearance, just as abbreviate the quantity of years expected to grow a Christmas tree to showcase size.

Contingent upon species, site and the board rehearse, it takes six to twelve years to deliver an attractive Christmas tree. Harvests with a long revolution like Christmas trees ought to never be developed without first knowing the underlying soil fruitfulness levels and amending any evident nutrient insufficiencies preceding planting, as estimated by an ongoing (inside a half year prior to planting) soil test.

After trees are planted, it turns out to be extremely hard to apply soil corrections and successfully join them with culturing. Proposals gave by this reality sheet are planned to urge Christmas tree producers to apply most soil fruitfulness contributions, except for nitrogen (N), prior to planting. These suggestions are a blend of soil fruitfulness research in New Jersey, and encompassing states, just as from functional experience of business Christmas tree cultivators.

Despite the fact that N is a basic nutrient for Christmas tree production, N proposals are not founded on soil testing. Plant tissue examination, in any case, might be a helpful instrument to manage N applications. In the time of planting, N manure is not suggested. Subsequently, this reality sheet initially talks about nutrient suggestions and soil pH the board that depend on soil testing.

Proposals for phosphorus (P) and potassium (K) shift contingent upon the underlying soil richness test level.

Soil pH and liming proposals, nonetheless, are more species explicit. The most regularly developed species for the greater part of the climate might be gathered into two general soil pH inclination classes. An objective soil pH of 6.0 is suggested at season of planting for Norway tidy, Fraser fir, Canaan fir, Scotch pine, and white pine. For Douglas fir, blue tidy, and concolor fir the objective soil pH is 6.5. Despite the fact that these species may like, or can endure, to some degree lower soil pH levels, these objective soil pH levels are suggested as beginning stages at starting planting time, since soil pH normally diminishes during the pivot. Utilization of compost materials likewise gradually drives down the dirt pH. Whenever trees have been planted nutritional alterations must be applied to the foliage or soil surface; there is no occasion to work corrections into the dirt until the finish of the turn.

BEST VARIETIES TO GROW BECAUSE OF THEIR VALUE AND ACCEPTANCE

- **Resin fir**

In the event that what you need most is the it-must-be-Christmas smell when you stroll in the entryway, the Farmer's Almanac says this is the most fragrant of the Christmas tree varieties.

It has a solid, 'hot' Christmas tree aroma and its tapered structure and dim green shading cause it what a great many people to relate to as a Christmas tree. It additionally has astounding needle maintenance! Its delicate green leaves are a top pick for wreaths.

- **Douglas Fir**

One of the top Christmas trees in the United States, as per The National Christmas Tree Association, Douglas Firs are well known in light of their ideal pyramid shape. Additionally, since they transmit needles every which way, Douglas Firs will in general be overall quite full. While not a genuine fir, Douglas can be found on each tree ranch. With dull green or blue-green shaded needles that are delicate to the touch and a sweet aroma, Douglas firs hold solid as a top pick. Be cautioned, however this tree will drop its needles on the off chance that it does not get enough water.

- **Fraser Fir**

For the individuals who like to go all-out with embellishments, the Fraser Fir may be the smartest option. The needles are delicate to the touch and yet its branches are hardened and will hold up well to decorations. It has a decent evergreen fragrance and needle maintenance is magnificent.

- **Colorado Blue Spruce**

The allure of the Colorado Blue Spruce is, as its name recommends, its blue or shiny appearance, ideal for a snowy front room. Blue tidy has firm branches with sharp needles. It is ideal to wear long sleeves when taking care of and beautifying. On the off chance that you have meddlesome pets, this might be a decent decision as the bothering from the needles will ordinarily fend them off. As indicated by the Farmer's Almanac, it has great needle maintenance, as well.

- **Canaan Fir**

Canaan Firs are frequently portrayed as being fundamentally the same as the Balsam Fir, however with the additional needle maintenance of the Fraser Fir. "It is a relative 'newcomer' in contrast with different Christmas tree species. It has a thick pyramidal shape like Fraser and amber fir, and its needles will in general bend upward.

- **White Spruce**

The National Christmas Tree Association says these are incredible for trimmings since they have short, hardened needles. "They have fantastic foliage tone and have a decent, characteristic shape. Simply don't get it for the smell. The needles are pale blue green, yet they have an unsavory smell when squashed.

- **White Fir**

Likewise called the Concolor Fir, this tree has been picking up in notoriety. "It has a charming blue or green shiny shading and the needles when squashed have a lovely citrus smell. It likewise has phenomenal needle maintenance.

- **Norway Spruce**

This Norway Spruce model was so quintessentially Christmas, its enhanced Rockefeller Center in 2015. "Norway tidy is alluring for its sobbing, pendulous structure as a Christmas tree. Yet, needle maintenance is not generally excellent except if the trees are cut new and kept watered.

- **Scots Pine/Scotch Pine**

The Scots Pine (or Scotch Pine) is known for its more obscure green/somewhat blue green tone, which says something in a front room. "Scots trees have an enduring smell. Furthermore, you do not need to stress over losing needles on the off chance that they are kept very much watered.

- **Eastern White Pine**

These are ideal on the off chance that you are going for a characteristic look and need the tree to be simply the concentration in and; as indicated by The National Christmas Tree Association, they are not incredible for adornments and have little fragrance, but rather the delicate, adaptable needles sure are beautiful. "The white have basically no aroma, making it a top pick for the individuals who have touchy noses.

- **Easter Red Cedar**

With needles that stream straight upward, Eastern Red Cedars are especially thick and green. In spite of its name, it is not really a cedar tree, it is actually a piece of the juniper family.

CHRISTMAS TREE SEEDLINGS AND TRANSPLANTS

Great Christmas Trees originate from great seed. Great seed originates from developed and improved seed plantations. A research body chosen the best trees from their first revolution of Balsam Fir mountain strain, cooks' strain, and Balsam X Fraser half breeds to create prevalent seed. They picked this seed in fall when it was ready. They dried and put away the seed until the spring planting season.

In the spring after they did germination tests, they planted the seeds at rate to get a thickness that produces great quality seedlings. The entirety of their seed was planted on extraordinarily built raised beds. Beds were concealed for first year, which gets them looking great so far. The seedlings were developed on for a very long time turning out to be 2-0 seedlings.

In Fall of the second year they lifted the 2-0 seedlings. They evaluated out the best seedlings and replanted them into transplant beds. Subsequent to planting they mulched the entirety of their transplant beds in pre-winter, to assist them with establishing in better. They fill on in the transplant beds for 2 additional years turning out to be 2-2 transplants.

When the 2-2 transplants have finished growing, they lifted and evaluated out their best transplants for their clients to handle plant for Christmas trees.

SELLING CHRISTMAS TREES

1. Discover a Supplier (Tree Farms)

- To begin a Christmas tree business, you need a provider that can get you trees in mass.

- In any case, where do individuals purchase their Christmas trees in mass?

- Tree ranches! - That is correct, the best spot to purchase Christmas tree in mass and modest is a tree ranch.

- Also, to discover a ranch close to you, you should simply do a couple of searches on web.

Use terms like:

- Christmas tree discount close to me

- Christmas tree ranches close to me

Whenever you have discovered a ranch or two, make certain to get some information about their mass estimating. Look at the statements from a couple of various ranches and go with the best one.

2. Pick a Lot

This is the part a great many people may have a few issues.

- On the off chance that you own a great deal some place where there is a high foot or vehicle traffic, at that point you are brilliant.

- On the off chance that you do not claim a ton, you should lease one. Costs fluctuate from area to area.

- For the most part, you need a great deal that is effortlessly observed and can be gotten to rapidly and effectively too.

- Parking garages of huge squares and even significant retail establishments are probably the best spots. You can get individuals while they are in their vacation shopping temperament.

Obviously, it will not be anything but difficult to lease such spots. Fortunately, it is conceivable. Others are doing it. It just takes a little work.

3. Prepare Your Tree Lot

- Presently you have your discount provider and you have an obvious part in an incredible area.

- The subsequent stage is to make your parcel appear as though it is the spot to purchase Christmas trees.

- There is truly not a lot to do here but rather to coordinate your trees in slick lines dependent on estimate and enhance a portion of the trees.

In any case, there is one thing missing!

- You just have trees. You have to add a couple of more things – wreaths and a couple of different occasions related handcrafted things.

- Having those couple of additional things will assist with expanding your deals. It adds visual interest, and sometimes, that is all you require to change over an "I'm simply perusing" shopper to an "I'm getting it at the present time" client.

4. Market the Heck out of Your Christmas Tree Selling Business

- Finding a high traffic territory can get you most of the way there.

- Yet, on the off chance that you need to truly bring in cash, you need to spread the news.

o   Facebook posts

o   free Craigslist promotions

o   announcement sheets of the nearby basic food item and retail establishments

o   Verbal exchange

o   Promotions in nearby papers

o   Flyers

There are huge loads of approaches to showcase your business. Think outside about the container.

TIPS TO INCREASE SALES

At the point when Christmas Day is close, similar to a couple of days away, bring down the costs of your trees.

Another approach to expand your income is to offer delivery administrations for the trees. The trees are pretty colossal and it is difficult for certain individuals to bring them home.

Purchasers will at that point be paying special mind to delivery administrations and you could have trucks to move the trees back to their homes without a moment to spare for Christmas.

MAKE SOMEBODY'S HOLIDAY SPECIAL

On the off chance that you have extra trees that did not sell, you can give them to poor and penniless families.

Not exclusively will you fulfill these families during the Christmas season, it will likewise spare you from paying the expenses for the removal of the trees.

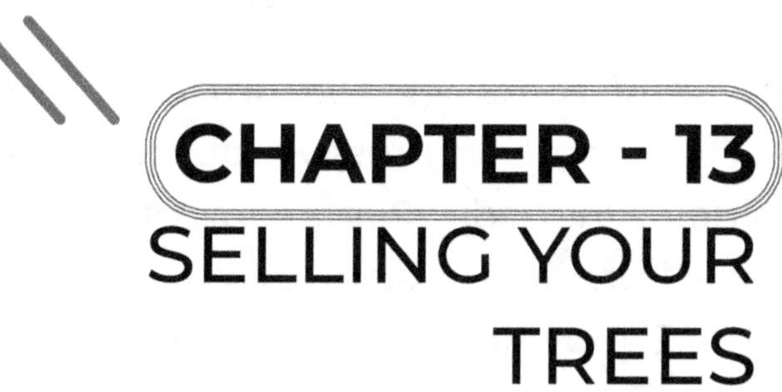

CHAPTER - 13
SELLING YOUR TREES

APPROACHES TO USE SOCIAL MEDIA TO PROMOTE YOUR TREE CARE BUSINESS

Searching for an approach to get the message out about your tree care business? With the correct blend of instruments, online media can take your business higher than ever to assist you with transcending the opposition. Here are only a couple approaches to utilize online media to advance your tree care business.

Make fruitful ground with a blog - You have heard it previously and you will hear it 1,000 additional occasions: Content is the best! Reliably sharing incredible substance is key for directing people to your site and building brand steadfastness, so consider making a blog where you can impart important data to your intended interest group, for example, occasional tree care tips and counsel.

Seed your substance through online media - One of the most ideal approaches to advance your substance is through the various web-based media channels accessible to your business, for example, Twitter, Facebook, LinkedIn and Google+. Zero in on making network around your substance by building a connected with crowd that is eager to like, offer and most loved your substance.

Fabricate solid roots with informal - Word-of-mouth is as yet the most impressive approach to advance your business. Indeed, 92 percent of individuals trust suggestions from loved ones over some other type of showcasing. Exploit advanced verbal exchange by urging fulfilled clients to get the message out through online media, and watch your clients begin drawing in with others as they show their being a fan.

Develop your business with Facebook - With 1.49 billion dynamic clients, Facebook is currently greater than the biggest nation on Earth, which makes it an easy decision when considering instruments to expand mindfulness about your tree care business. The most ideal approach to draw in your crowd on Facebook is to make a Facebook page and update it routinely with convenient, important and significant data focused to your crowd.

Branch out to new channels - Once you have aced Facebook, consider spreading out to new channels where your crowd is effectively partaking. For instance, Google+ and LinkedIn both offer exceptional business benefits. LinkedIn is an extraordinary method to interface with your Back to Back audience, and Google+ offers site improvement

(Website design enhancement) and neighborhood SEO advantages to assist clients with finding your business on the web. Site improvement is the way toward improving the positioning of a site in an internet searcher's unpaid outcomes, and neighborhood SEO is the advancement cycle for nearby outcomes in web crawlers.

Online media is a significant instrument for your business, yet it is imperative to remember, similarly as growing and thinking about a tree takes arranging, association and great dynamic, so too does keeping up a viable web-based media presence.

Notwithstanding, the universe of web advertising is one that keeps on growing step by step. It is significant for individuals in any sort of business to execute these showcasing procedures. Administrations that cannot be given carefully ought to consistently zero in on nearby outcomes.

Remember that your promoting endeavors should be steady. Regardless of whether you figure out how to accomplish a decent position or increase a huge after, you will not keep up it on the off chance that you quit making content and drawing in with different clients.

CHAPTER - 14
SETTING GOALS

PRUNING AS A CASE STUDY!

A few trees are more confounded; others are more managed down in scale.

A few trees have a couple of various issues going on, and all need thought in framing a last system prior to pruning starts.

What is essential to recall is that pruning is not just an undertaking for general tree upkeep.

At the point when you employ an organization to manage back the trees on your property, it assists with telling your master tree expert what you are attempting to accomplish. The team would then be able to set goals, plan system and carefully consider factors that will differ from zone to territory, site to site, for example, the age of the trees, the species, where they are found, and so on Your data causes them to do the most ideal work.

These destinations stream down, and impact different choices in the pruning cycle. Setting up a tree administration with however much data as could reasonably be expected better sets it up to deliver a phenomenal outcome!

HERE ARE EIGHT ZONES PRUNING AS A GOAL SETTING CAN ADDRESS:

Diminishing danger - This would be an instance of tree decay, illness or rot that could make an appendage fall and cause injury or harm, or appendages that are scouring toward one another, debilitating the tree itself.

Basic enhancements - Pruning in a manner that considers better separating of the branches, swarmed trees are troubled trees.

Rebuilding pruning - This is the point at which we prune trees to reestablish a view, sight line, or direct them to fill such that will not meddle with things like utility lines.

To oversee size/shape - Some land owners like their trees more proportional with different highlights of their territory or might want a tree more modest to permit more daylight in.

Regenerative pruning - Tree specialists will prune back old wood to clear a path for new shoots, carrying energy to new pieces of the tree.

To improve feel - This is a sort of tree pruning that hoists a tree's visual allure; customary support is ideal to keep your trees looking extraordinary.

To oversee production - Fruit trees and botanical trees can profit by particular pruning to make more fruit or blossoms in less time.

To oversee untamed life - Possibly a National Park needs more than typical shelter or tree cover to shield a winged creatures' home from hunters. Or then again you have a territory in a lawn tree you are hoping to keep flawless. All things considered; we would leave more shelter inclusion in view of that thought.

Correspondence with your tree administration is vital to getting the goals of your pruning venture achieved.

UTILIZING THE 80-20 RULE IN THE GARDEN

Italian financial analyst Vilfredo Pareto was an energetic gardener.

He saw that 20% of the pea pods in his garden contained an astounding 80% of the general peas.

He applied this intriguing finding to his financial aspects work and found that about 20% of the individuals in Italy possessed about 80% of the land.

From that point forward, this marvel has been archived in numerous zones, particularly in the business world (for instance, 80% of an organization's business originate from only 20% of its clients).

It has been named the Pareto Principle, or the 80-20 guideline for short.

Incidentally, it is regularly the situation that 80% of the outcomes you get from any endeavor will originate from only 20% of the exertion you put into it.

That is a staggeringly valuable principle to recollect whether you are the sort of individual who needs to streamline your life or even be more successful at how you deal with your time.

On the off chance that you can figure out what that immeasurably significant 20% is, you can spare yourself a great deal of time.

Truly, in the event that you are attempting to develop nutrient-thick food, it is a test to separate that into only a couple steps, particularly in the event that you are beginning with helpless soil.

But then, there are several significant things you can do in the garden that can have a gigantic effect.

CHAPTER - 15
BUSINESS BASICS

MONETARY AND TAX ASPECTS OF TREE PLANTING

Trees are planted for some, reasons, including landscaping, soil and water preservation, natural life environment, and nut and wood production. Philanthropy propels numerous landowners to plant trees. There are, nonetheless, the individuals who plant with the desire for expanding their family's riches. The attention is on trees planted for business lumber production. Different purposes, for example, landscaping, are referenced to recognize their treatment with the duty treatment of trees planted for business wood production. Interior Revenue Code and related specialists are referred to for charge experts.

MONETARY ANALYSIS OF TREE PLANTING

The monetary ramifications of the long time-frames associated with recouping tree planting costs and acquiring an adequate pace of degree of profitability are critical. Cash spent on tree planting may not be returned by the offer of lumber products for quite a long time. Much of the time the expense is borne by one age and the pay got by a later age. In the event that you do not anticipate getting pay from a tree planting venture during your lifetime, it is essential to inquire as to whether planting trees is monetarily legitimized. This is less significant if tree planting ventures are seen as a multi-generational action, or will expand the honest assessment of the property.

Choices likewise can be seen in more extensive cultural terms, i.e, will society advantage in the event that you plant trees, or would it be smarter to contribute your resources on some other venture?

The conventional method to dissect venture alternatives is to lead point by point limited income examinations (DCFA). DCFA gauges the net present value of a task utilizing a predetermined elective pace of return, or gauges the pace of return really procured by the venture, alluded to as the inward pace of return.

DCFA expects you to gauge costs and incomes numerous years into what is to come. You additionally need to assess lumber development rates, number of trees per section of land, wood value, and greatest years to gather, among numerous different suspicions.

TREES AND INSURANCE COVERAGE

As winter ice storms offer approach to spring and summer twisters, which offer approach to fall typhoon season, there will never be a terrible chance to find out about restricting the budgetary misfortunes brought about by tree harm to your property. What is covered? What isn't? How might you limit your misfortunes?

Many shade and fancy trees are harmed during the time

by windstonns, lightning or ice and snow collections. Harm for the most part comprises of a couple of broken branches. Be that as it may, more serious harm, for example, parting or pulling separated of branch associations, expulsion of enormous zones of bark, curving and parting of the storage compartment, or in any event, removing present potential perils.

Homes or assets harmed because of a fallen tree, regardless of whether it is your tree or a neighbor's tree are commonly covered under your mortgage holder's insurance strategy.

In certain circumstances where the brought down tree was on a neighbor's property; your insurance organization may attempt to gather from a neighbor's insurance organization if the tree was in chronic frailty or not appropriately kept up. In the event that the safety net provider is effective, you might be repaid for the deductible.

The expense to eliminate fallen trees might be covered if:

The tree was removed due to windstonn or fell after a lightning strike;

The tree harmed a structure, for example, a carport or shed; or

The tree missed the house yet obstructs the carport or impediment access ways.

Your trees, shrubs, plants or yard are commonly not covered from harm. Vehicles harmed by flotsam and jetsam or fallen trees are covered under the "other-than-impact" (otherwise called "thorough") part of a collision protection strategy. This is discretionary inclusion that secures safeguarded vehicles in circumstances other than a crash or upset. On the off chance that the gauge demonstrates extreme climate ahead, vehicles should be moved under cover to keep harm from high breezes or flying flotsam and jetsam.

CHAPTER - 16
HELPFUL RESOURCES
FOR TREES GROWER

SECRETS OF SUCCESSFUL TREES GROWER

With nurseries limiting their plants by 30 to 50 percent, fall is an extraordinary chance to purchase and plant trees.

When planting a tree, it is imperative to burrow an opening multiple time the width of the root ball and no more profound than the root ball itself. You will likely get these headings when you purchase the tree. Nonetheless, there are some fine focuses for planting container-developed trees that directions oftentimes do not specify. So here they are:

Search for the root flare at the lower part of the tree trunk - The root flare is the zone of the storage compartment that is somewhat more extensive than the remainder of the storage compartment. Here and there cultivators will conceal the root flare in the container so the storage compartment appears as though a utility pole right to the dirt. On the off chance that you don't see a more extensive region at the lower part of the storage compartment, delicately eliminate the dirt in the container until you see the root flare.

Subsequent to eliminating the tree from its container, score the sides of the root ball in the wake of eliminating the pot - This implies making 3 to 5 vertical cuts into the root ball around 1 inch right from the base edge of the root ball to about halfway up. At that point run a hand cultivator along the root ball evenly to pull the roots from the root ball so they will develop out into the dirt and assemble nutrients as opposed to proceeding to develop around the root ball. This is called root lightening.

On the lower part of the root ball, make 1 to 2 cuts 3 to 4 inches down - Check for supporting roots, that is, enormous roots growing around and around the root ball.

Supporting roots can destabilize the tree and inevitably kill it - On the off chance that you discover a supporting root, cut it and check whether you can pull the rest of the root so it will become away from the plant. On the off chance that you cannot, remove the supporting root totally. On the off chance that it would seem that all the enormous roots are supporting roots that cannot be fixed, consider returning the tree to the nursery. In the event that you got it on special, however, you might be trapped.

Check the profundity of the opening to ensure the root flare is even with the dirt review or up to one inch over the dirt evaluation. In the event that you plant the tree too profoundly, water will gather in the downturn around the storage compartment, making the roots decay.

Whenever you have put the tree in the planting opening, turn it so the best side of the tree faces the heading from which it will be seen regularly.

Eliminate any labels from the tree. As the tree develops, labels can go about as a tourniquet, delving into a branch.

Subsequent to filling in the planting opening, trim any suckers from the base of the tree prior to mulching and watering the tree.

CONCLUSION

There is a ton to consider when planting a tree and if all else fails, connect for the experience and ability of a talented expert.

A tree, when planted and cared for appropriately can turn into a deep-rooted expansion to your property. In like manner, if not done appropriately will build the requirement for support and other exorbitant issues later on.

Nonetheless, growing high-value trees on a tree ranch can carry a lot of higher benefits to cultivators. Start-up costs are low, and request is growing each year.